Baby Apes

Bobbie Kalman

Crabtree Publishing Company
www.crabtreebooks.com

It's fun to learn about Baby Animals

Created by Bobbie Kalman

Dedicated by Louise Mayer
To my beautiful granddaughter, Abigail Charise Pretty,
who fills my life with pride and joy. I love you.

Author and Editor-in-Chief
Bobbie Kalman

Editor
Robin Johnson

Research
Crystal Sikkens

Design
Katherine Kantor
Samantha Crabtree (cover)

Production coordinator
Katherine Kantor

Illustrations
Barbara Bedell: pages 7, 9 (bottom), 11, 20, 24
Katherine Kantor: page 14
Bonna Rouse: page 9 (top)
Margaret Amy Salter: page 6

Photographs
iStockphoto.com: back cover (chimp), pages 9,
    10 (top right)
© Shutterstock.com: cover (background), pages 1, 4, 6,
    7 (right), 8, 10 (bottom left), 12, 13 (bottom right),
    18, 19 (bottom), 20, 21, 22 (left), 23 (top left),
    24 (all except feelings, groups, and habitats)
Other images by Creatas and Digital Vision

Library and Archives Canada Cataloguing in Publication

Kalman, Bobbie, 1947-
    Baby apes / Bobbie Kalman.

(It's fun to learn about baby animals)
Includes index.
ISBN 978-0-7787-3948-7 (bound).--ISBN 978-0-7787-3967-8 (pbk.)

    1. Apes--Infancy--Juvenile literature. I. Title. II. Series.

QL737.P96K29 2008   j599.88'139   C2008-900140-0

Library of Congress Cataloging-in-Publication Data

Kalman, Bobbie.
    Baby apes / Bobbie Kalman.
        p. cm. -- (It's fun to learn about baby animals)
    Includes index.
    ISBN-13: 978-0-7787-3967-8 (pbk. : alk. paper)
    ISBN-13: 978-0-7787-3948-7 (library binding : alk. paper)
    ISBN-10: 0-7787-3967-8 (pbk. : alk. paper)
    ISBN-10: 0-7787-3948-1 (library binding : alk. paper)
    1. Apes--Infancy--Juvenile literature. 2. Apes--Juvenile literature. I. Title. II. Series.

QL737.P96K24 2008
599.88'139--dc22
                                                     2007052901

Crabtree Publishing Company

www.crabtreebooks.com   1-800-387-7650

Published in Canada
Crabtree Publishing
616 Welland Ave.
St. Catharines, Ontario
L2M 5V6

Published in the United States
Crabtree Publishing
PMB16A
350 Fifth Ave., Suite 3308
New York, NY 10118

Published in the United Kingdom
Crabtree Publishing
White Cross Mills
High Town, Lancaster
LA1 4XS

Published in Australia
Crabtree Publishing
386 Mt. Alexander Rd.
Ascot Vale (Melbourne)
VIC 3032

What is in this book?

What is an ape?

An ape is an animal called a **mammal**.
Mammals have hair or fur on their bodies.
Apes have hair on their bodies. Mammals are
born. You were born. You are a mammal, too.

*This is a **newborn** gorilla. It is only a few days old.*

Mammal mothers feed their babies milk. The milk is made inside the bodies of the mothers. Drinking mother's milk is called **nursing**. This baby chimpanzee is nursing.

Apes or monkeys?

monkeys

Apes and monkeys look similar, but they are not the same. Monkeys have tails. Apes do not have tails. Most apes are bigger than monkeys. Are the animals in the picture below apes or monkeys? Why do you think so?

These animals are monkeys. They are small animals with long tails.

There are many kinds of apes. Gorillas, chimpanzees, and orangutans are three kinds of apes you will see in this book.

Chimpanzees are also called "chimps."

Gorillas are the biggest apes.

Orangutans are reddish brown in color.

Ape bodies

Apes have two arms and two legs. Their arms are longer than their legs are. Most apes use their arms and legs to walk. Some apes walk on their feet and on the **knuckles** of their hands. Walking like this is called **knuckle-walking**.

Other apes can walk on two legs.

Apes have hair on their bodies.

*Apes have **backbones** inside their bodies. Backbones are the bones in the middle of an animal's back. Animals with backbones are called **vertebrates**.*

Apes do not have tails.

Apes have five toes on each foot.

Apes have five fingers on each hand.

knuckles

All mammals must breathe air to stay alive. You breathe air using **lungs**. Lungs are body parts that take in air and let out air. Apes also breathe air using lungs. You can see a gorilla's lungs in this picture.

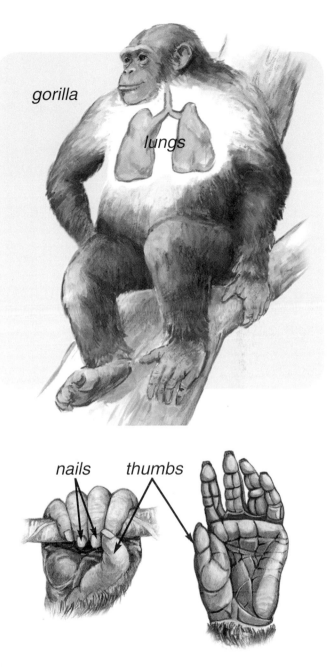

gorilla

lungs

nails   thumbs

Apes have a thumb on each hand and foot. Thumbs help apes hold on to objects such as tree branches. Apes also have nails on their fingers and toes. Apes use their nails to pick up small things.

This baby orangutan has long fingers!

Hairy apes

Orangutans have long red hair and dark gray skin. The hair of male orangutans is longer than the hair of female orangutans.

Male orangutans have large cheeks.

Chimps have black hair. Some chimps have light skin. Other chimps have dark skin. Chimps have large ears and small **nostrils**. Short white hairs grow from their chins.

nostril

a silverback

Gorillas have small ears and large nostrils. Young adult male gorillas have black hair on their backs. They are called **blackbacks**. As the gorillas get older, their back hair turns silvery gray. Older males with gray hair are called **silverbacks**.

What do apes eat?

Most apes eat mainly plants. Apes eat leaves, flowers, seeds, and roots. They love fruit! Some apes eat both plants and animals. They eat insects and other small animals.

Gorillas eat mainly plants. This baby gorilla is eating branches and leaves.

Apes need both food and water to stay alive. They get a lot of water from the plants they eat. Apes also drink water from streams and puddles. Sometimes they put their hands into water and then drink the water that drips off their hands.

This orangutan is drinking the water that drips down from its hand.

Chimps eat both plants and animals. This chimp is eating an insect. Chimps use tools such as sticks to get the insects they eat.

This baby orangutan has some food in its hand. What kind of food do you think it is?

Where do apes live?

The natural places where animals live are called **habitats**. Most apes live in **forest** habitats. Forests are habitats with many trees. Most apes live in habitats that are warm all year long. Some gorillas live in forests high up on mountains. The weather is cool in these forests.

Gorillas spend time on the ground as well as in trees.

Chimpanzees live in warm forest habitats. They spend time in the trees and on the ground. This baby chimp and its mother are resting high up on a tree branch.

This young chimp is climbing a tree.

Life in the trees

Orangutans live in **jungles**. Jungles are hot forests with many trees. Orangutans eat, sleep, and play in the trees. They build **nests** in the trees, too. Nests are beds made from branches and leaves. Orangutans sleep in the nests and cover them when it rains.

Orangutan mothers teach their babies how to climb and swing from tree to tree.

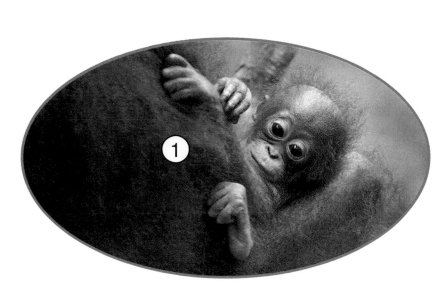

1. At first, baby orangutans hold tightly to their mothers.

2. This baby can now hold on to a tree by itself.

3. "Oh, no! That is a long way down!"

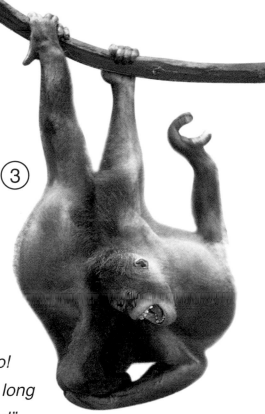

1. This young orangutan is now climbing and swinging on its own.

Ape families

Apes have different kinds of families. Most apes have one baby at a time. Some baby apes live with only their mothers. Other babies live with their mothers and fathers. Some apes live together in large groups. Others live on their own.

Baby chimps live with their mothers in groups. These chimpanzees are part of a larger group of chimps.

Gorillas live in troops.

Some apes live in large groups called **troops**. Troops have a few males, some females and their babies, and some young apes.

Baby orangutans live with their mothers. The mothers teach their babies how to climb trees and find food. Male orangutans live alone.

19

Growing up

Apes go through changes as they get older. These changes are called a **life cycle**. Apes start their life cycles when they are born. Their bodies change as they grow. Over time, the apes become adults. These pictures show the life cycle of a gorilla.

Newborn gorillas are very small.

Baby gorillas drink milk from their mothers.

Adult gorillas can make babies.

Young gorillas like to play.

When a baby gorilla is strong enough, it rides on its mother's back. The baby gorilla is safest when it is close to its mother. When the baby is three to four years old, it stops nursing. It lives on its own, but it stays in its mother's troop. At the age of eleven, a male gorilla leaves to find its own troop.

Showing feelings

Apes share their feelings with one another. They use sounds such as hoots, screams, grunts, and songs to show how they feel. They frown, bang their chests, and stomp their feet when they are angry. Apes also hug and kiss a lot.

Are these chimps hungry, or are they happy?

This angry gorilla is hitting its chest. It is trying to scare away an enemy.

This mother gorilla is kissing her baby.

This baby orangutan is kissing its mother.

These chimps are hugging each other.

I wonder what this baby is thinking!

Words to Know and Index

backbone

bodies
pages 4, 5, 8-9, 20

chimpanzees
pages 5, 7, 11, 13, 15, 18, 22, 23

feelings
pages 22-23

food
pages 12-13, 19

gorillas
pages 4, 7, 9, 11, 12, 14, 19, 20, 21, 22, 23

groups (troops)
pages 18, 19, 21

habitats
pages 14-15

hair
pages 4, 8, 10-11

life cycle
pages 20-21

orangutans
pages 7, 9, 10, 13, 16-17, 19, 23

Other index words
families pages 18-19
mammals pages 4, 5, 9
mothers pages 5, 15, 16, 17, 18, 19, 20, 21, 23
nursing pages 5, 21
trees pages 9, 14, 15, 16, 17, 19
vertebrates page 8

Printed in the U.S.A.